Bob-Lo Revisited

Bob-Lo Revisited

PHOTOGRAPHS BY BILL RAUHAUSER

HISTORY BY MARTIN MAGID

Press Lorentz

ANN ARBOR / CHICAGO

Other books with photographs by Bill Rauhauser:

The Family of Man
Detroit Revisited

ART DIRECTOR Eliza Wilson-Powers
PUBLISHING DIRECTOR Jude Wilson

Design: Eliza Wilson-Powers

Published in 2003 by Press Lorentz, Ann Arbor/Chicago

ISBN 0-9723926-0-2
Library of Congress Control Number: 2003106153

Printed by University Lithoprinters, Inc., Ann Arbor, Michigan.

Press Lorentz

931 Hockey Lane
Ann Arbor, Michigan 48103
www.presslorentz.com

PRINTED IN USA

This book is dedicated to
my friend in photography,
Robert R. Wilson.

Bill Rauhauser at Bob-Lo, 1941
photo by Doris Lippert

Doris Lippert (Rauhauser) at Bob-Lo, 1941
photo by Bill Rauhauser

THE PHOTOGRAPHS IN THIS BOOK of Bob-Lo Island and of the excursion boats, *Ste. Claire* and *Columbia*, were made over a period of forty years. There was no grand plan to document the Island or to produce a record of a day on the river or at the Island. I simply enjoyed taking photographs with my Leica. From the moment I boarded one of the boats waiting at the dock, the trip down the Detroit River past the industrial plants lining the shore, the activity on board, including dancers enjoying "Indian Summer", "In the Mood", and other wonderful tunes of the thirties and forties played by the ship's band, as well as other activities on board, all offered a wonderful opportunity to take pictures. Arriving at the island opened up even more picture possibilities as people enjoyed themselves on the amusement rides and in the picnic areas and paid little attention to a man with a small camera.

Asking a young lady for a date was much easier if it was to be at Bob-Lo. Dancing on the boat seemed so romantic and the Island was full of fun things to do. My first visit to Bob-Lo was with a date and while it was a wonderful day, I realized going alone would give me more freedom to photograph as dating and photography did not always mix.

Because there didn't seem to be a good opportunity to exhibit these photographs, over time I boxed them up and stored them in my closet. The closing of the Island in 1993 and the bicentennial celebration in 2001 of Detroit's founding seemed to present an opportune time to bring them out of the closet and publish them. They might serve as a catalyst to remind Detroiter's who made Bob-Lo a frequent summer outing– and all those from around the country who were occasional or even one-time visitors– of the wonderful times Bob-Lo provided; first as a child with their parents, later on a first date, then with their own children, and finally as seniors enjoying a warm day on the river.

All who ever enjoyed a delightful trip to Bob-Lo Island aboard the *Ste. Claire* or the *Columbia* excursion boats will understand my sorrow on boarding the *Ste. Claire* in the fall of 2002 and seeing its present state. The steamer that had sailed so proudly up and down the Detroit River for almost a century had fallen into a devastating state of decay. These few photographs can only partially remind us of its past glory.

But as the French photographer Brassai tells us in his book, *Proust in the Power of Photography*, this is what the camera does best:

> *...in his battle against time, that enemy of our precarious existence, ever on the offensive though never openly so, it was in photography, also born of an age-old longing to "fix" it forever in a semblance of eternity, Proust found his best ally.*

Bill Rauhauser

April 2003

On The Boats

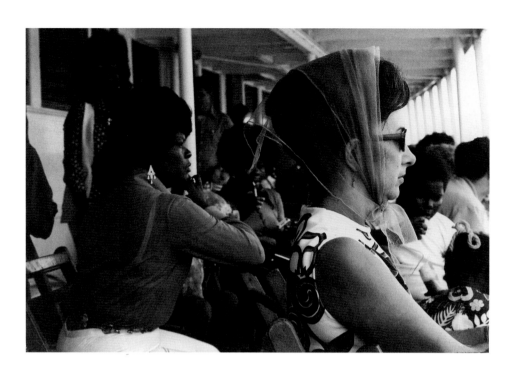

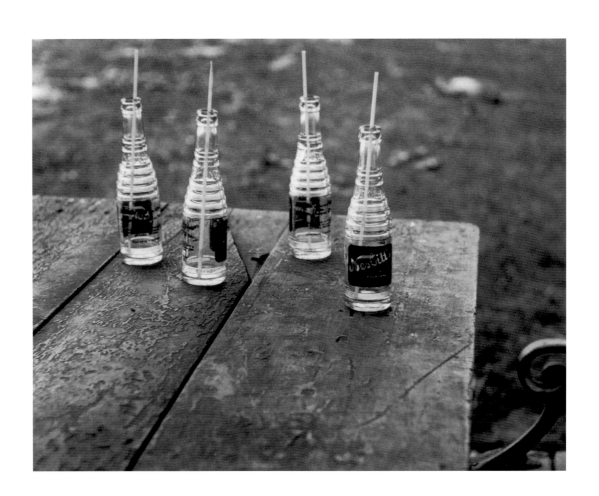

The Island

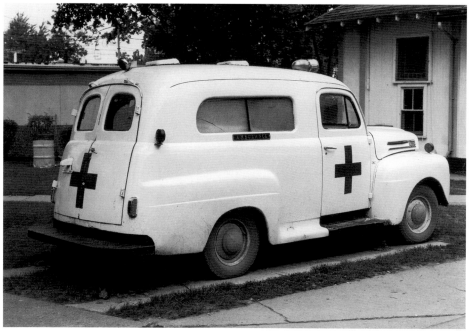

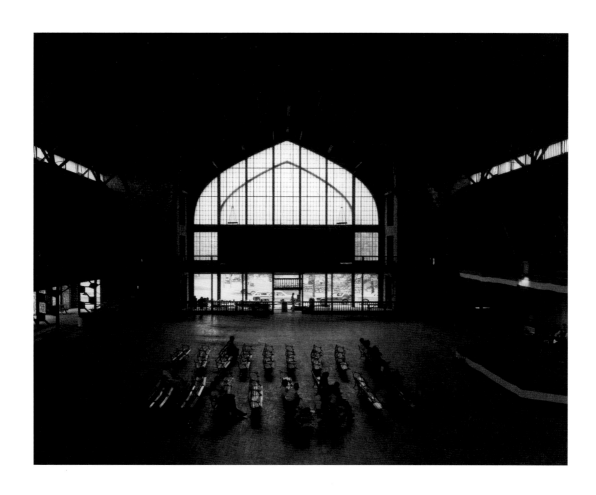

Going Home

THIS WAY OUT

Bob-Lo Island: Detroit's Canadian Jewel

HISTORY BY MARTIN MAGID

This Bob-Lo history is dedicated to the memory of my parents, Ben and Ann Magid, who introduced me to the boats and the Island.

It is also dedicated to my wife, Sue Beale, and our children, Steve Majid, Gary Magid, Linda Magid, Mark Henderson and Annie Magid-Beale, who gave me the opportunity to visit Bob-Lo and introduce them to its pleasures.

– Martin Magid, April 2003

Introduction

> Detroit is going to have a new summer resort to be known as Bois Blanc Park. It is on Bois Blanc island, which is 19 miles from this city, off Amherstburg....Bois Blanc Park is no hastily constructed, indifferent amusement ground, but has been carefully selected with reference to its accessibility, scenic effects and general utility. Since early spring it has been in the hands of large gangs of men who have been making every effort to preserve and add to the natural beauties of the island, by such permanent improvements as art and taste can suggest. [1]

Ever since the Detroit, Belle Isle & Windsor Ferry Company announced an expansion of its service to include new excursion trips from Detroit, the whole city had waited in excitement. The new excursions would take passengers from Detroit to the beautiful and spacious picnic grounds on Bois Blanc Island, down the Detroit River. Church groups and other organizations booked passage on the boats and reserved picnic space on the Island. The *Detroit Evening News* and the *Detroit Tribune* bought all the tickets for a first voyage on the steamer *Promise* for the annual newsboys outing. On that day, Monday, June 20, 1898, the boys got a day off from school for the occasion.

Realizing that "boys will be boys," the boat operators ran the following reassurance in the evening newspaper: "The services of Capt. Ed Horn have been secured for the occasion, and special arrangements have been made for the safety of the little fellows. Row boats with expert swimmers will be towed behind to provide against possible accidents." [2] The paperboys left the dock at 8:00 am and their parents and brothers and sisters followed on the *Sappho* an hour later, dressed in their finest for the auspicious event. Mrs. Martha Walpole recalled that first boat trip in a newspaper article, "I had to wear my new dimity dress and stand beside my folks. My father wore a black coat and stiff white collar. My mother had on her best dress." [3] That Monday departure in 1898 launched the glorious, fun-filled years of Bob-Lo Amusement Park, lasting 95 years—until September 26, 1993.

Prior to 1898, Bois Blanc Island's neighbors a few hundred feet away in Amherstburg, Ontario, picnicked on the Island, and so did large groups by charter. The distance was too great for regular use by Detroit-area residents. When the ferry opened the Island to Detroiters, a good-natured dispute arose over the pronunciation of the Island's name. Few Detroiters could pronounce Bois Blanc as the French do, and they usually massacred the name by saying "Boys Blank." Captain Walter A. Campbell, head of the ferry company, respected tradition and tried to educate the public, but with little success. A limerick, popular at the time, illustrated the point:

> A maiden once said to her Pa,
> "Oh Pa, can I go to Bah Blah?"
> Her father said "No!
> You can't go to Bob-Lo,
> The place is too terribly far!" [4]

Captain Campbell gave up after a few years, and everyone eventually used 'Bob-Lo,' including the ferry company. The Canadian government officially changed the Island's name to "Bob-Lo" in 1949.

"On the beautiful island they called 'Bois Blanc' ("White Woods"), about seventy Indian men and their families lived peacefully, raising crops on fertile land." So wrote an anonymous traveler in 1718. The memoir provides one of the oldest surviving eyewitness descriptions of the narrow two-mile long island at the mouth of the Detroit River.

The first European settlers came in 1742. The Jesuit "Mission of the Assumption of the Blessed Virgin Mary Among the Huron" moved from Detroit to Bois Blanc Island. Jean Baptiste Goyeau, his wife and six other Frenchmen worked the Mission farm with help from the Indians. Goyeau was the first European farmer in what became the Province of Ontario. Five years later rebel Hurons attacked the Mission. They wounded three settlers, and five Indians were captured. The attack was part of a widespread uprising against the French in the Ontario-Michigan-Ohio region. A Huron woman, a household worker inside Fort Detroit, learned of the uprising and informed the authorities. The warning saved Fort Detroit and minimized the effectiveness of the attack on the Mission. The Mission relocated to the present site of Assumption Church in Sandwich, Ontario, and full control of Bois Blanc Island returned to the Indians.

When the British finally left Detroit in 1796, thirteen years after signing the treaty ending the Revolutionary War, they moved downstream and built Ft. Malden in Canada across from Bois Blanc Island. Over 500 Indian families used the Island as their campground when they spent time trading furs to the British at Ft. Malden. During the years following the Revolutionary War, armed conflicts arose between pro-British Indians and Americans settling in Ohio, Michigan and Indiana. The Shawnee brothers, Tecumseh and Prophet, led the campaigns for the Indians. The Americans destroyed Prophet's village at the Battle of Tippecanoe, and the Indian survivors fled in late 1811 to Ft. Malden. The Indians camped on Bois Blanc and were fed by the British through the winter.

When the War of 1812 broke out, British Major General Isaac Brock visited Tecumseh on Bois Blanc and rallied his warriors to the British cause. Tecumseh stopped frequently at Bois Blanc while visiting Ft. Malden during the War. He was killed at the Battle of the Thames in 1813. The Treaty of Ghent ended the War in 1814, but it did not resolve border issues regarding Bois Blanc Island. Eventually both sides agreed that the King of The Netherlands should resolve the territorial disputes. In 1831 he ruled that Bois Blanc Island was part of Upper Canada and would remain an English colony.

The birth of the line of ferry boats traveling the Detroit River to the Island took place in 1820. François Labaleine, "Francis the Whale," took passengers across the river.

> He had a six-foot-long horn hanging from a tree on each side of the river. And when a passenger wanted to cross the wet half-mile from Detroit to Windsor, or vice versa, he just blew on "Francis the Whale's" mighty horn. You had to have a lot of breath on a windy night to travel from Windsor to Detroit back in the 1820's.[5]

Construction of a lighthouse began on the south end of Bois Blanc Island in 1837. The people of Amherstburg wondered who would get the plum job as lighthouse keeper. One day Sir Francis Bond Head, Governor of Upper Canada, saw a beautiful Newfoundland dog in Amherstburg, and asked if he could buy him. The owner said she could not possibly sell the family dog, but if her husband became lighthouse keeper, she would give the dog to Sir Francis. Mrs. James Hackett's hard bargain provided steady work at the lighthouse for her husband and for successive generations of Hacketts for over one hundred years.

The 57-foot height of the lighthouse allowed the lamp to beam 18 miles to river and lake traffic. Originally, the lighthouse "was a 10 lamp burner with 8 of the lamps facing toward the Lake and 2 upstream. Down through the years, various improvements were made…acetylene gas replacing the oil lights and later electric. In the fall of 1954, vandals broke in and set a fire which destroyed the lamp house top structure."[6] Although the Canadian government decommissioned the lighthouse in 1959, it still owns and maintains the several surrounding acres.

During Canada's Patriot War in 1838, American soldiers captured Bois Blanc Island and held it for less than one day. The Patriot War involved French sympathizers, the "Patriots", against the English. A group of Patriots and Americans attacked Ft. Malden with an old cannon hauled on the schooner *Ann*. American General Sutherland invaded Bois Blanc with 300 soldiers to assist the *Ann's* contingent. When rifle fire from Ft. Malden cut the halyard, and her mainsail fell, the schooner foundered and drifted downstream, finally settling on the Canadian shore. The English captured the *Ann* and her entire crew.

General Sutherland watched the battle and the *Ann's* final humiliation from the safety of Bois Blanc. He withdrew his men back across the river, ending official American participation in the Patriot War. Ft. Malden's commander ordered the island's trees cut down for an unobstructed view of the American channel of the Detroit River. That deforestation is largely to blame for the disappearance from the island of the "white woods" for which it was named.

Following the Patriot War, the Canadian government strengthened defenses around Amherstburg. In 1838, it built three identical, exceptionally strong two-story blockhouses on Bois Blanc, one each at the north and south ends and one in the middle. They were built to effectively defend against attackers on the ground while minimizing exposure by the defenders. On Canada's Confederation Day in 1867, revelers dismantled the north blockhouse and used the wood for a bonfire.

The only other military skirmish on Bob-Lo Island (the island's official name after 1949), more than a century later, found Americans and Canadians on the same side during the weekend of October 18, 1958, after the park had closed for the season. At the height of the Cold War, some had great fear about the Soviet Union's ability to attack North America with ballistic missiles. Military reserve training exercise "Operation Bob-Lo" presumed Detroit was hit with an atomic bomb. Reserve troops on Grosse Isle near Bob-Lo were evacuated. "Enemy" paratroops landed on Bob-Lo, and a force from Grosse Isle counter-attacked by helicopter and rubber raft. The Essex and Kent Scottish Regiment of Windsor and Chatham, Ontario, swept down one side of Bob-Lo, and the U.S. Marines from Brodhead Armory in Detroit advanced down the other. Marine Sergeant Raymond Wawrzynski was evacuated by helicopter as a casualty, but not before he and his crew gained an unexpected prize: one of them reported, "We even got ourselves a prisoner last night. We talked a sergeant from Toledo right out of his machine-gun."[7]

Around the middle of the 19th century, Colonel Arthur Rankin, a Member of the English Parliament, purchased 225 acres of Bois Blanc Island from the Canadian government. He paid forty dollars in total. Notwithstanding the low cost of real estate in those days, the favorable price likely reflected Colonel Rankin's position. Captain James Hackett, the lighthouse keeper, held the remaining 14 acres of Bois Blanc in a lifetime lease. Col. Rankin's son, the New York actor Arthur McKee Rankin, purchased the property from his father in 1869 for a summer home and possible development as a resort with a hotel

and cottages. Arthur McKee Rankin converted an abandoned military blockhouse into an elegant home, built stables and stocked the Island with Shetland ponies, deer, wild turkeys, peacocks and elk. A steam-powered yacht, the *Kitty B.*, named for his wife, shuttled Detroit and out-of-town guests between the Island and Amherstburg. "It was a great summer gathering place for New York's actor colony. Mr. Rankin was a lavish host. The Delmonico crowd was there in numbers watching their amiable host play one of the most realistic roles in his entire career, that of the gentleman sportsman."[8]

Rankin over-spent at a time when his theatrical career was declining, and he lost the island property to the mortgage company in 1877. The prominent Detroit lawyer John Atkinson and his friend and business partner James Randall purchased the 225 acres for an amount estimated to be at least $40,000 and perhaps as much as $100,000. Randall, known as "the father of Detroit's boulevard system," laid out streets and cross-streets on the property. The partners announced plans for a 100-room hotel, but this development, like that planned by the Rankins, never reached fruition. The close friendship and partnership of Randall and Atkinson ended in a bitter quarrel, and Atkinson demanded that Randall dismantle a home he had begun on the acreage. Randall refused to stop construction, and refused to sell out to Atkinson. One morning residents discovered the structure torn down and the site became known as "Randall's wreck." The estranged partners eventually divided their island property. Randall kept four acres on the north end and Atkinson retained the remainder. Randall sold his acreage to William Menzies, who built a summer resort hotel in 1909. The resort did well until Menzies sold it in 1913.

The Park Opens and Prospers

In 1897 the Detroit, Belle Isle and Windsor Ferry Company approached John Atkinson about leasing some of his acreage on the Island. They wanted the lease to be for a period of time long enough to give the recreational enterprise a chance to catch on with Detroiters. They signed a 15-year lease for the 25 acres at the northern end of Atkinson's property, with an option to purchase the property at the end of the lease. As it turned out the Ferry Company's business-like caution was unnecessary. Detroit's new summertime playground prospered immediately. By the time it closed 95 years later, the park's facilities had expanded several times over, and the Bob-Lo company owned the entire island except for the lighthouse area, which the Canadian government retained.

Picnics near the the river after the boat ride were the main activity when the park first opened to the public. Though the younger set preferred the amusement rides which came in the years ahead, the family, church, lodge and company picnics were the main attraction for their parents. The record for the largest crowd at a Bob-Lo picnic was held for many years by the Border Cities Retail Merchants Association for its 1921 event, attended by 10,000 people. The wedding of Winnifred Mahey to William Shelton was a main event on that day. Not surprisingly, the new Mrs. Shelton won the prize for "best appearing lady." Other prizes were given for best baby, largest family, a pie-eating contest, a tug-of-war, running races, ball throwing, cracker eating and much more.[9] Picnics through the years replayed the events of this one day.

One of the earliest written records of activities on the Island involved dancing by visiting Indians. Twenty-two-year-old Isaac Weld, Jr. visited Ft. Malden for the first time in the fall of 1796 and kept a journal of his travels. Just before midnight on his first night at the fort, Weld heard the sounds of Indian drums. He and his friends paddled across the river to the Island and found the assembled Indians. Men played instruments and sang, and both men and women danced, but never together. The Indians walked, leaped and spun around, stomped on the ground with great enthusiasm, and at the end of the dance they all shouted in unison. Weld and company joined in the festivities, though perhaps with some trepidation. He later wrote: "There is something inconceivably terrible in the sight of a number of Indians dancing thus around a fire in the depths of thick woods, and the loud shrieks at the end of every dance add greatly to the horror which their first appearance inspires."[10]

Over a century later, dancing on the Island was no less popular. The ferry company built an indoor dance pavilion for the 1898 opening. By 1901, the owners doubled the capacity of the original dance floor. A new cut stone dance pavilion opened for the 1913 season, boasting the largest dance hall in North America. Dancing cost five cents per couple, and a second-floor gallery provided a view of the whole dance floor. The dress code prevented admission of men with suspenders and women wearing shorts. Captain Campbell allowed only the regulation two-step or waltz—no "freak dancing," no rags, ping-pongs (a "wriggling version of the couchee-couchee"), turkey trots, bunny hugs or bear dances.

A large new restaurant opened right on the water for the 1901 season. The owner left nothing to chance in designing this facility. A short description was printed in the *Amherstburg Echo* in March of that year: "Mr. Campbell made a tour of the seacoast watering places, and seeks to combine all the improvements in those he saw, in this cafe. It will be large and handsome, surrounded entirely by verandas, while the interior will be a cafe, with all the modern improvements, in charge of a first class chef. The building will be connected to the Island by a dock, and the whole will be lighted with electricity."[11] This announcement represented a remarkable reversal of Mr. Campbell's original vision for the park. Three years earlier, he said the park would not be electrified because it was not for "the night owls." This change undoubtedly recognized the phenomenal success of the Bob-Lo venture and the potential for additional revenue.

Facilities on the Island included swings and teeter-totters, baseball diamonds, and tennis courts. In the early years the swimming beach roller coaster-type ride took swimmers on a noisy track and made a big splash into the water. A golf course opened on the Island's north end in 1925. Although golfing was popular, attendance dwindled with the Depression, and the course closed in 1937. A Vernors ginger ale factory also opened in 1925, a small ferris wheel and a miniature "Brownie Coaster" in 1930, and, in 1963, a marina for 180 pleasure craft of all sizes on the west (the American) side of the Island. Gary Sodini recalled:

> My wife's employer had a big Chris Craft boat and every summer he took all his employees on the boat and parked at the Bob-Lo marina and stayed there all day. It was very relaxing, you could go to the amusement park, then go back to the boat to rest, then go back to the park. We spent all day there, morning to night.[12]

The true beginning of the Island as an amusement park had begun with the arrival in 1906 of the Mangels-Illions carousel and pipe organ. William F. Mangels, a legend in the industry, manufactured the frame in his Coney Island, New York, factory. Marcus Charles Illions, a master craftsman of "the Brooklyn school", designed and hand-carved the 48 animals and two chariots for the carousel in his Brooklyn, New York, workshop in 1878. Of the 44 horses, no two were alike, and all had gold-leafed manes. The carousel was painstakingly restored in 1987, each animal requiring between eighty and one hundred hours of work.[13] Kids often got an especially long carousel ride, sometimes more than they wanted. In an Amherstburg history, Janet Botsford McBride remembered:

> Landing on the island, we ran for the merry-go-round which was situated away south. Here Mr. Mc Caffrey would start up the engine and ride away on his bicycle giving five or six youngsters an hour's free ride. We always chose an outside horse as that provided us the greatest thrill. Long before the hour was up we were ready to get off. No matter how enjoyable, one can get too much of a good thing![14]

Low attendance because of the Depression and competition for cross-river traffic from the recently completed Ambassador Bridge (1929) and Detroit-Windsor Tunnel (1930) significantly reduced the ferry company's income; it closed Bob-Lo operations for the 1933 and 1934 seasons.

The Detroit, Belle Isle and Windsor Ferry Company planned new amusement park attractions and added Toledo and Monroe as pickup locations for 1935, but the ferry company sold the business in 1939 to the Chicago, Duluth and Georgia Bay Transit Company. The new owners changed the name to The Bob-Lo Excursion Company, Ltd.

The timing was right for the new Bob-Lo company as the country finally emerged from the Great Depression. The number of visitors to the Island increased dramatically and very large crowds sometimes made it difficult to get everyone quickly to and from the Island. A group of Sunday schools arranged a charter for 3,200 women and children to go to Bob-Lo on June 9, 1941. Ten thousand people showed up, and although the boats managed to get them to Bob-Lo with several trips, getting them all back at the same time was impossible. Anxious parents waited for their children at the Detroit docks and panicked when there was no employee available to deny a rumor that a Bob-Lo boat had sunk. Well after midnight, thousands of children returned, shivering on the open boats.

The number of adult amusement rides increased from six just after World War II to 27 by 1957. Another growth spurt from 1969 to 1974 saw the addition of a super slide, spiral drop, flume ride, Tilt-A-Whirl and the Sky Streak roller coaster. In 1983 AAA Michigan purchased the island, park and boats and invested $5 million in improvements for the 1986 season. They installed the Sky Tower with its slowly rotating 20-mile view into Michigan, Ohio and Ontario, added a second train for the Screamer Corkscrew roller coaster and added a fourth boat for the Gibraltar/Bob-Lo trip which in 1985 proved popular beyond expectations. The park stayed open on weekends through the end of September with pickups at Amherstburg and Gibraltar.

The park's last roller coaster was installed in the late 1980s inside the dance pavilion building. The "Nightmare" sped through darkness on a 1,150-foot track at 35 miles per hour. After this conversion of the dance pavilion building, dancing was an option only on the Bob-Lo boats. The opening of a 4.5 acre zoo and petting farm in 1969 permitted a waggish columnist to report in the liberated '70s that everyone knew the "real" petting farm was at the top of the ferris wheel.[15] The miniature train passed through the African-motif village, populated by 300 exotic animals and birds, including a giraffe, a lion, and a cheetah. There were also chimpanzees, baboons, deer, antelope, lambs, goats, llamas, donkeys, geese, ducks and a 200 pound tortoise for the kids to ride. The zoo brought a set of problems previously unknown on Bob-Lo. In the first year, a photographer placed a white duck near Leo the Lion for a group photograph. When the zoo director and the photographer turned away for a moment, the duck disappeared. That's when Leo got his tether. Seven baboons escaped in 1972 for two days. They were all recaptured, but one baboon holed up in the funhouse and it took patient coaxing to get him out.

The Bob-Lo Boats

The transformation of Bob-Lo from a quiet spacious picnic ground into a rollicking full-scale amusement park and zoo meant little to many who rode the boat only for the smooth serene ride itself, rather than the destination. Many people took the boat ride several times a year and never set foot on the Island. Jack Harris spoke of the days when he courted his future wife, Kathleen Graff:

> Once a year I would leave work in Pontiac, still wearing my coat and tie, and drive to Grosse Pointe to get Kay at her office, and we headed for the Bob-Lo boat. We always stopped at the Women's City Club on the way to pick up a picnic basket for dinner on the boat. It was a very respectable thing to do in the summertime, everyone was on their best behavior. We loved the boat ride, and never got on the Island. We just stayed on board and returned to Detroit. We did that every year.[16]

Just boarding the boat in Detroit was an exciting experience. There might be time to rush up Woodward Avenue for burgers at the White Tower, or a Vernors cream ale at the corner of Jefferson Avenue, under the huge Vernors sign that was a beacon for seamen. Better to do it before the picnic because the parents were usually too tired to do it after the boat ride back to Detroit. In the early days, horses and carriages dropped families off at the foot of Woodward. Detroit police at the scene served as more than just traffic control. Former Officer Fred C. Rickert recalled in a newspaper article: "People would be all excited about going on the boat to Bob-Lo Island Amusement Park. When they were walking down the steep hill from Jefferson Avenue and the boat whistle would sound, they would start running, thinking that the boat might leave without them. Their fruit (plums, apples, pears and peaches) would start falling out of their baskets. We would assure them that the boat would not leave without them, and then we would assist them in retrieving the fruit."[17]

And it wasn't only the passengers who ran for the boats. Concession employee Jane McCraight-Wertz recalled: "I usually reported for work at seven in the morning for the eight o'clock boat. One day I stopped for breakfast at a McDonald's, and that was a mistake because they were really slow. I had to run for the boat just as they were pulling the ramp away and the boat was creeping away from the dock. Without even thinking about it, I jumped across the opening. It was like being in a movie."[18]

"Captain Bob-Lo" entertained the crowd as they gathered to board. He was played by Joe Short, a clown hired away from the Ringling Brothers Circus where he had played "Little Joe from Kokomo." Short was also in the movie versions of the comic strips "Katzenjammer Kids" and "Mutt and Jeff." During the Christmas shopping season, Joe and his wife Louise dressed as Santa's helpers at Kern's Department Store in downtown Detroit. He also marched in parades as Captain Bob-Lo and appeared as a cowboy at circuses and the Michigan State Fair. Short's performances as Captain Bob-Lo had no set schedule. He worked when he wanted to, and no one told him how to do his job. Entertaining kids was his specialty and he knew that very well. The four foot four inch entertainer worked the Bob-Lo dock and boats until 1974, when he was in his nineties. When word spread during that year that Captain Bob-Lo was hospitalized and had no visitors, hundreds of well-wishers mobbed the hospital. Joe Short died Christmas Eve of 1974. Members of the Detroit Fire Department Clown Team served as his pallbearers.[19]

Many steamships sailed the Bob-Lo line in the early days, including the *Promise*, *Garland*, *Pleasure*, *Britannia*, *Scotia*, the *Papoose* of the first few years and the *Papoose* of the 1970s, the *C.H. Park* and the *Sappho*. But the best remembered and the most loved are the *Columbia* and the *Ste. Claire*.

The *Columbia* was launched from Wyandotte, Michigan, in 1902, and the *Ste. Claire*, built in Toledo, joined the line eight years later. Sometimes called "the people's yachts," both are U.S. National Historic Landmarks. The *Columbia* carried up to 2,566 passengers and the *Ste. Claire* 2,414. The Coast Guard required that each

of them carry a "navigating crew" of 35, who slept on the boats and worked in shifts. The crew included the captain, first and second mates, wheelsmen, lookouts, deck hands, engineers, oilers and wipers. It did not include the concession employees, musicians or other entertainers.[20]

The *Columbia* and *Ste. Claire* had second deck dance floors and live music most years, replaced by juke boxes toward the end. Beer gardens were on the third deck. There were, of course, food concessions and the obligatory souvenir stands. "Mollie Bulver stood behind her souvenir stand on the second deck of the good ship *Columbia* and surveyed the boxes of tin trombones, blue and white captains' hats, and 50-cent monogrammed plastic Bob-Lo back scratchers stacked around her. 'Oh, it'll all be gone by tomorrow night. We usually don't have much surplus when the season ends.' "[21]

When each boat slid slowly from the dock the band would play "Anchors Aweigh." The *Pleasure* and the *Promise* made the first trips in 105 minutes, and in 1902 the *Columbia* raced to Bob-Lo in 80 minutes, reaching sixteen miles per hour. Patrons on the boats ran up and down between the first, second and third decks, ate, drank, or listened to the music. Looking down into the engine room and watching the engine's powerful, monotonous thrust was a popular fascination. Dancing and watching dancers were also popular pastimes and the captain's prohibitions were strictly enforced. An early remembrance in a 1906 scrapbook describes the results of misbehavior on the dance floor:

> Last year, Samuel Meisner was put off the *Columbia*. His friend Niederlander was removed
> from the dancing floor for indulging in an obscene dance (the rag). Meisner intervened, and
> nearly came to blows with the Purser. Meisner was denied passage a week later; he tried again
> this summer, was refused, then sued. The Purser demonstrated the dance in court, and the
> court blushed.[22]

The sights along both the Canadian and American shores changed greatly through the years. In that first summer of 1898, only small buildings appeared here and there. Later the buildings got bigger and taller, and the passengers watched the construction of the Ambassador Bridge as it stretched its way across the river. Great industrial complexes grew on both shores as the steel, automobile and chemical companies expanded in and around Detroit and Windsor. Watching freighters pass with their flags and names from all over the world, and exchanging arm waves with the deck hands while the captains exchanged blasts on their steam whistles became a tradition on the Detroit River.

The lights of the city and the Ambassador bridge sparkled on the moonlight cruises. Romance prevailed and evening dancers crowded the floor. The Jack Okie and George Smith Orchestras provided dance music in the late 1930s, and Frank Gilbo and Joe Vitale led their orchestras for many years on post-World War II evenings. On Friday nights in 1980, big bands formerly led by Harry James, Woody Herman, Count Basie, Bob Crosby and Tommy Dorsey played their famous signature themes.

The Friday and Saturday moonlight cruises were known by some employees as a "floating bar." Ralph Browning of Lincoln Park, Michigan, managed the concessions on the boats for 30 years. He recalls a busy night when the bartenders were pouring a lot of liquor: "A well-juiced patron told a bartender that he was going to jump overboard. The bartender told him 'I'm too busy for that. Go on downstairs and do it.' The man did just as he was told, he jumped off the stern on the second deck. We had to stop the boat and turn around, but we did rescue him." [23]

Mrs. Isabel Stachura felt fine on the day of the annual Bob-Lo picnic of the Polish Women's Alliance in 1923, despite her advanced pregnancy. She sold tickets for the club at the dock and danced on the *Columbia*. But once on the Island, she knew she had better head straight back. She almost made it back— the baby emerged when the *Columbia* passed the stacks of the Great Lakes Steel Company, nearly to Detroit. The First Mate assisted with the delivery of Caroline Columbia Stachura. Called Columbia all her life, Ms. Stachura received a lifetime pass from the Bob-Lo company on her sixteenth birthday. "I'm proud to be named after the *Columbia*. The *Columbia* has always been my favorite boat and Bob-Lo has always been one of our favorite places. We always went on the *Columbia* and the crew would usually give us– all my cousins and aunts and uncles– a cabin to use." [24]

Most years, smaller boats ferried passengers between Amherstburg and Bob-Lo. But once a year the nearest residents got to ride the big boats.

> [E]ither the *Columbia* or the *Ste. Claire* was chartered locally for an excursion from Amherstburg in July. The scene was lifted straight out of Stephen Leacock's *Sunshine Sketches of a Little Town*: a band playing, the ship's whistle blowing, mothers calling, children screaming and the ship stuck in the mud at the dock until a McQueen tug could arrive to pull it free. A memorable time was had by one and all! [25]

The installation of "the Great Lakes' Most Unique Dock" preceded the 1961 season. The hull of the old Canadian freighter, the *Queenston*, was sunk in place to form the new dock. The landscaped deck became a walkway to the Island on a wide canopied promenade. Once the boat landed, the kids either galloped to the rides or found the best picnic spot for the rest of the family. Mrs. Wilbert Fox remembered in a newspaper article, "I used to win all the foot races we had on the Island, and since I was the fastest it was my job to race off the *Promise* and grab the picnic table before anyone could get it." [26]

A Multinational Island

As season attendance approached its peak in the mid-1970s, Bob-Lo Island resembled a small city, with its own water treatment plant, waste disposal facility and fire and rescue departments in addition to all the amusement and dining facilities. Students from an Amherstburg high school and the University of Windsor comprised most of the 400 employees. Labor problems were few, but habitually late paychecks caused a short strike in 1942. The company learned its lesson and paid on time the rest of the season.

One employee suffered a particularly bad run of luck over a period of three years. In August 1945, thieves assaulted Fred Nester, a night watchman from Windsor, and took $10,000, the day's receipts. The next summer, six men rowed to the Island and robbed the cafeteria after hours, keeping Nester and three others under armed guard while they worked on the safe. In the summer of 1948, four armed bandits took a speedboat to Bob-Lo carrying sawed-off shotguns. They landed on the north end of the Island early in the morning. One of them slugged Nester as he was leaving the administration building and knocked him unconscious.

Residents of both countries know the U.S.-Canadian border as the most peaceful and the easiest for law-abiding citizens to cross. The Bob-Lo company, an American organization, ferried Americans and Canadians to a Canadian island while crossing the international boundary several times. Bob-Lo Island developed an unofficial multinational standing as the years went by. For example, while the U.S. in World War I prohibited draft age American men from leaving the country, the government relaxed its rule for Michigan men going to Bob-Lo. In the case of Anton Pernicka, the U.S. federal court refused to strictly apply the immigration statute to travel between Detroit and Bob-Lo. The statute of limitations prevented the U.S. government from deporting Pernicka for his illegal entry in 1923. However, if he left the U.S., he could not return. After his visit to Bob-Lo in 1928, he was arrested upon arrival back in Detroit. The court did not view his trip to Bob-Lo as "foreign travel," and permitted him to remain in the U.S.A.

In 1940 Canada was at war with Germany but the U.S. was still neutral. The F.B.I. discovered that members of the German Bund were fleeing from Canada to the U.S. via the Island. First, they ferried from Amherstburg to the Island (Canada-to-Canada). Once on the Island they bought return tickets to Detroit from the office manager on the Island. There was never any form of customs or immigration inspection of passengers arriving in Detroit from Bob-Lo. This method of travel was also used by Canadian shoppers between Canada and Detroit to avoid Canadian customs fees.

American immigration officials felt that the only way to stop the German nationals from illegally entering the U.S. through the Island was to terminate the Amherstburg connection. From 1940 to 1947, Canadians could get to Bob-Lo only by going to Detroit by bridge or tunnel, where they had to show a passport, then take the Bob-Lo boat to the Island. Canadians living near Amherstburg were especially unhappy about this turn of events. There is little doubt that the Bob-Lo company lost substantial revenue from them during those years.

From its beginning, the excursion company reserved the right to exclude "colored" people from its boats and the Island. Newsboy, and future mayor of Detroit, Eugene Van Antwerp rode to Bob-Lo on the newsboys cruise on June 20, 1898,[27] but Boy Scout, and future mayor of Detroit, Coleman Young was turned away in 1931 because he was African-American. The rest of his Boy Scout troop sailed without him to Bob-Lo on the *Columbia*.[28] The irony is that it is well known that Bob-Lo had provided a haven for runaway slaves as part of the Underground Railroad.

World War II created a new consciousness among many minorities when faced with unfair treatment. They began to resist. Sarah Elizabeth Ray worked as a civilian for the U.S. Army. In June of 1945, she and classmates in a training program planned a trip to Bob-Lo, sponsored by the Army. Thirteen of them gave their money to one of the group who then purchased tickets, and all went aboard. Before the boat left the dock, two employees of the Bob-Lo company approached Miss Ray, sitting in a deck chair with the others. She was the only African-American. They asked her to leave, and it was clear that it was because of her race. She refused at first, but saw that the employees were prepared to carry her off with force; she took names and filed a criminal complaint in Detroit against the Bob-Lo Excursion Company.

Michigan courts convicted the company of violating the state civil rights act and fined it twenty-five dollars. The company appealed to the U.S. Supreme Court, claiming its operations were "foreign commerce" and not subject to the Michigan statute. The Court found that, "[e]xcept for the small fenced-off portion reserved for the lighthouse and three cottage sites, the island is economically and socially, though not politically, an amusement adjunct of the city of Detroit."[29] The Supreme Court agreed with the Michigan courts: The Bob-Lo company must operate its excursion boats under Michigan law as "public conveyances," and accept persons of all races without discrimination. The decision was issued early in 1948. After the season ended the Bob-Lo Excursion Company announced it would not operate in 1949.

The prospect of the loss of Bob-Lo upset the people of southeast Michigan and the Windsor-Amherstburg area. A newspaper reporter wrote "Detroit would not be Detroit without its Bob-Lo and the excursion boats."[30] There was great relief and gratitude in the Spring of 1949 when Troy H. Browning, of Grosse Pointe Michigan, bought the amusement park and the *Columbia* and *Ste. Claire* and promised to open the new season in June. The Detroit City Council passed a Resolution commending Browning for keeping the operation going, and the Acting Mayor presented it to him on May 13, 1949.

Two corporations ran the new Bob-Lo enterprise. The Bob-Lo Company, a Michigan corporation, owned the boats. The Island of Bob-Lo Company, an Ontario corporation, owned the island and the amusement facilities. Over the years, the Bob-Lo Company sought groups for charter cruises from all neighborhoods and every kind of organization. Browning's Bob-Lo company ran charter cruises for groups of all religions and races, private companies, fraternities like The Varsity Club, union groups including the Trade Union Leadership Council, political fundraisers for Coleman Young and John Conyers, and the Society for the Preservation and Enjoyment of Barber Shop Quartets, which held contests on board. Troy Browning arranged a free cruise and a day on the Island for 2,500 youngsters selected by a juvenile court judge. In the peak years, new groups faced a waiting list for available cruises. The company also began to pick up passengers in Toledo, Ohio, but that was discontinued after a few months when the *Canadiana*, rented by Bob-Lo, ran into a bridge mistakenly lowered by the bridge operator.

Bad Publicity and Competition: The Decline

Steadily rising patronage over the years coupled with increased use of machinery for amusement attractions led to incidents which diminished Bob-Lo's reputation as a safe place, and played a part in its decline. In 1942, a teen-age girl drowned when she fell from the Bob-Lo gangplank. This was the first serious accident on Bob-Lo, and attendance suffered, but climbed back by the mid-1940s. The worst accident involving a ride was the first, on August 24, 1965. A rider on the "Bug" died and eight others were hurt when their car broke loose from its support and flew off the track. Newspapers raised the issue that no Ontario law dictated periodic safety inspections of the rides. Investigation determined that faulty metal was used to manufacture the support, but would have been undetectable even by standard Michigan inspection procedures. Nevertheless, newspaper photographs of the mangled ride and the injured passengers graphically illustrated the potential harm, and consequently attendance dropped temporarily.

The five-year period from 1973 to 1978 saw a high number of ride accidents, but no fatalities. In June 1973, a fifteen-year-old girl suffered back, neck and arm injuries when she was thrown from the "Wild Mouse." One month later, two young women were injured when thrown from the "Sky Streak" roller coaster. On the day before opening day in 1974, an employee walked across the track of a roller coaster and into the path of a car. Reporters present for "press day" made the accident a front page story. When a mother and child were hurt in a ride just over two weeks later, the press commented that Ontario still had no law or regulation requiring amusement ride inspections. Another pre-opening accident occurred in 1976 when the brakes failed on a test of the "Galaxy" roller coaster, injuring two employees. After the ride was repaired and opened to the public, a customer was thrown from the "Galaxy" at about the same point in the ride. 1977 was accident-free, but early in the 1978 season two thirteen-year-old girls fell from a swaying cable car and suffered cuts and bruises. Only one month later, the brakes failed on the "Sky Streak," injuring 10 passengers. The publicity from these events dramatically affected attendance.

Troy Browning and his brothers ran the Bob-Lo companies for continuous seasons from 1949 to 1979, interrupted only by the Detroit riot of 1967. In that summer the entire complement of Detroit police officers directing traffic at the dock was pulled and assigned to other areas of the city. The company's managers felt the boats were vulnerable to the destruction and arson that was going on over a large area of Detroit, so they sent the *Columbia* and *Ste. Claire* to Bob-Lo Island. They remained tied up for several days and operations were suspended for eight days total. However, even with that interruption 1967 was financially successful, and 1968 was even better.

After the 1967 riot, many Detroiters and suburbanites stayed away from amusement attractions in the downtown area of Detroit. Racial tensions were high, and many people did not feel safe or welcome in the city. In addition to the real or perceived safety concerns, the world-wide oil shortage of the late 1970s took its toll on the operation of the Bob-Lo boats. The number of trips permitted was severely curtailed. Even if patronage increased, the boats would not have been able to handle all the new passengers.[31] When the company's losses soared in 1979, Troy Browning sold the boats and the amusement park to Cambridge Properties of Kentucky. This new company ran Bob-Lo for only two years, and filed for bankruptcy in 1981. AAA Michigan purchased it in 1983, but sold it to the International Broadcasting Company in May 1988, just before Memorial Day.

The events of Memorial Day in 1988 caused serious damage to Bob-Lo's reputation, and forecast its end as a viable amusement activity. The company had sold boat ride and amusement park packages to two Detroit high schools which had rival gangs in their student bodies. Jane Davies-Culp, a supervisor of concessions on the *Ste. Claire*, recalled: "If the sales people knew anything about inner-city Detroit, they would not have scheduled kids from those two schools on the same boat. When we saw the schedule a week before Memorial Day, we knew there would be trouble."[32]

In the morning, the line at the ticket office at the Clark Street dock was a half-mile long. Ten thousand people, mostly youths, went to the Island. The morning boats were crowded, but peaceful. However, fights broke out on the Island all day, some of them gang-related and some involving knives; handguns were reportedly seen. The Ontario Provincial Police dispatched twenty armed uniformed officers to supervise boarding for the return trips to Detroit. All the kids wanted to stay at the amusement park as long as possible, which caused the late return trips to be extremely crowded. The fights which had begun on the Island continued on board the ships. Concession stands were looted and chairs and life jackets were thrown overboard. One captain sent a "mayday" call for police and the Coast Guard to meet the boat at the dock. When the *Ste. Claire* passengers saw the Detroit dock, they all tried to get near the exit. When the second and third deck passengers could not get down the stairways, they all rushed to the port side, nearest the dock, and the boat listed terribly. Fights near the gangplanks terrorized the crowd as it pressed to the exit.

Innocent bystanders had been caught up in frightening violence on the Island and on the returning boats. Jane Davies-Culp remembered reporting for work the next morning, "The first thing I saw was the fencing at the dock all torn up. It had to be replaced. We all knew that that was going to be the end of Bob-Lo."[33]

Many people inclined to visit an amusement park would hereafter think first of Cedar Point in Ohio, 2.5 hours from Detroit. There, violence was unknown and the rides were inspected and safe, and the most thrilling that technology could produce. Those who wanted peaceful picnic grounds could choose among the many parks in metropolitan Detroit or Windsor. However, those who desired a boat ride similar to the *Columbia or Ste. Claire*, but without fear of harm, had no place to go.

The Unthinkable Becomes the Inevitable

AAA Michigan had attempted to revive interest in Bob-Lo in the mid-1980s, but after the Memorial Day incidents of 1988 it was no use. The park operated for a few more years, but the decline continued. The International Broadcasting Company paid $20 million for the Island and the boats and planned to revitalize the enterprise, but attendance and revenue continued to fall. The cash-flow situation forced the company to auction the Mangels-Illions carousel. The carousel was, by this time, over 100 years old and keeper of some of the most sentimental memories for the park's oldest patrons. It was announced a fiberglass merry-go-round would replace the carousel. People came to the February 24, 1990 auction from as far as England to bid on the carousel animals and chariots. People also came just to say "so long" to old friends. Barbara Campbell of Trenton, Michigan, went to see the horse she rode every season for 37 years:

> 'Buddy' -- that's what I always called him -- probably knows more about me and my problems than anybody. I'd be the tallest person in line, and sometimes I'd have to wait a couple of times to get him, but it was worth it. Now, I don't suppose I'll ever go back. Who could tell their problems to a plastic horse?[34]

At $23,000, Buddy was beyond Campbell's reach. She teared up and kissed him goodbye. The auction brought in $824,000, but the sale of the original carousel further reduced the park's popularity, and attendance continued to plunge. Attendance dropped to 270,000 for the entire 1991 season, compared to nearly 800,000 in peak years. Labor Day of 1991 saw the last Bob-Lo trips for the *Columbia* and the *Ste. Claire*. The Bob-Lo company declared bankruptcy after the 1991 season. For the 1992 and 1993 seasons, patrons had to take the smaller ferries from Amherstburg, Ontario, or from Gibraltar in Michigan, to reach the Island. There was no service from Detroit or Windsor, the areas with the largest potential customer base.

Although it was announced that 1992 attendance increased to 317,000, it was widely believed that more than half of the customers attended on free passes from various merchants. Bob-Lo was purchased in February 1993 by the Nathan Capital Company, of Seattle. The sale price had dropped steeply from the $20 million paid by International Broadcasting only five years earlier to $3.7 million. Amusement park operations resumed in 1993, but closed on September 26 of that year. Planning began for a 1994 season, but all rides and other equipment were finally auctioned in the spring.

Gary Sodini owns a combination frozen custard stand and miniature golf course in Chesterfield Township, Michigan. He has vivid, pleasant memories of Bob-Lo, and wanted a memento of it on his business site: "We bought a bunch of stuff from Bob-Lo Island. We called them when we heard they were closing down and asked about things we could use for our miniature golf course. We went and found the two swans, eight totem poles, a spinning wheel and an orange loop and a bull's-eye from the Bob-Lo miniature golf course. We got a bunch of their putters and scorecards, and gave out the scorecards as mementos. We had about a thousand, and about a hundred pencils. We got everything for two thousand dollars the week before the auction. The swans have been recognized a couple of times. Older folks come by and recognize them from the Tunnel of Love. Just two nights ago a guy came by and recognized the swans."[35] The swans lie on Sodini's golf course, in good shape and filled with beautiful flowers.

Employees also held similar sentimental attachments to Bob-Lo and the boats. Jane McCraight-Wertz worked at concessions and in the dock office from 1984 to 1986 and again in 1991, and remembers: "Employees tended to be either a *Ste. Claire* person or a *Columbia* person. I worked on both but I was a *Ste. Claire* person. We worked every other day, from 7 am to 2 or 3 am the next day. Two or three times a year all the concession people and the boat crews, the deck hands, maintenance people, purser and so on, would go to Belle Isle after work. The deck hands would play softball in the middle of the night, the *Ste. Claire* against the *Columbia*, and the rest of us would cheer for our favorite boat. They were the best summers of my life."[36]

The *Columbia* and *Ste. Claire* were both sold at auction on January 17, 1996. Two heritage foundations acquired them with plans to restore and preserve them, but they languished and deteriorated in their berths in Ecorse, Michigan. Diane Evon, formerly of Dearborn, Michigan, and her husband, John Belko of Cleveland, purchased the *Ste. Claire* on September 10, 2001, and had it towed to its birthplace in Toledo the next day. Mr. Belko and Ms. Evon have restored several old homes. When Mr. Belko learned the boats were for sale, he took his wife to see them. They saw that the boats were in deplorable condition from exposure to the weather and vandalism for 10 years, but they believed that the *Ste. Claire's* structure was solid, more so than the *Columbia's*.

When I saw the *Ste. Claire* in 2002 it had extensive water damage, missing planks and no floor at the bow. Vandals had ransacked the pilot house and stolen the compass and steering wheel. The electrical system was largely inoperable. Ms. Evon and Mr. Belko acknowledge they cannot afford to get the *Ste. Claire* into sailing condition. In the late 1970s the Bob-Lo Company spent over $300,000 between seasons on carpentry work on the *Ste. Claire* just to keep it in good condition.[37] Getting it into good shape today, starting from its current state of deterioration, would cost far more. Ms. Evon and Mr. Belko plan to eventually put it into sufficiently good condition to make it attractive as a venue for weddings and other celebrations.

On September 1, 2002, the *Ste. Claire* was towed from its slip to the dock at Independence Park in Toledo where it opened to the paying public on September 15, 2002 as the "Nautical Nightmare." As of October 2002, Ms. Evon was well satisfied with attendance. Due to popular demand, the *Ste. Claire* opened for daytime tours on the weekends.[38] Early in the summer of 2002 photographer Bill Rauhauser and I visited the boat at its home in Toledo. We climbed all over the *Ste. Claire* while a worker's radio loudly proclaimed Bob Dylan's "The Times They Are A-Changin'". Everyone hopes the times are changing for the better for the *Ste. Claire*.

People who attended meetings of the Friends of the Bob-Lo Boat *Columbia* reported in 2002 that members had not agreed on a course of action or a plan to improve its condition. Some insisted on restoration to its original sailing state. Others who saw difficulty in raising the funds necessary to accomplish its full restoration preferred something else that would make it accessible to the public who remembers and loves it. Meanwhile, a New York City maritime preservation group submitted a proposal to the National Trust for Historic Preservation to restore the *Columbia*, and to operate it as an excursion vessel on the Hudson River. When the Friends of the *Columbia* learned of the New York group's plan, it quickly put together a proposal and submitted it to the National Trust.

The National Trust was empowered to decide ownership of the *Columbia* because a loan made by the Trust to the Friends had been in default for several years. On January 8, 2003, the National Trust notified the Friends that its proposal was denied, and that ownership of the *Columbia* would likely be transferred to the New York group. The National Trust's decision was influenced by the failure of the Friends, over a seven year period, to raise the funds necessary for the extensive rehabilitation required. A representative of the National Trust explained that because the *Columbia* is a National Historic Landmark, it is better for the nation to have it restored and in operation elsewhere in the country than crumbling in Detroit. The timetable has the *Columbia* sailing on the Hudson River by 2005.[39]

The Island Today

The Royal Proclamation of 1763 issued by King George III granted title to Bois Blanc Island to the Walpole Island First Nation, the aboriginal tribe in possession at that time. The Proclamation permitted the tribe to sell the Island only to the King, for fair compensation acceptable to the tribe. On May 1, 2000, Canada's Indian Claims Commission held that the First Nation never voluntarily relinquished its title to the Island to the Crown, and failed to receive just compensation when other tribes unlawfully gave title to private persons. Therefore, according to the Commission, the Walpole Island First Nation still holds aboriginal title to the land.[40] However, Canadian law seems to protect third parties like John Oram who purchased most of the Island in 1994 with the assurance the title is clear. On the other hand, Walpole Island Chief Joseph Gilbert claims Oram paid for stolen property.[41] At this writing the matter rests with the Ontario Provincial Court, with a trial expected in 2003. If the First Nation prevails, it will likely own only the acreage surrounding the lighthouse.

John Oram purchased the Bob-Lo property with plans to develop nearly 300 homes and a commercial district, and to reopen the nine-hole golf course. By July 2002, 70 people lived on the island's north end in new homes, and a 37-unit apartment building was nearing completion. The ferries *Crystal O* and *Courtney O*, named for Mr. Oram's daughters, operate year round between Bob-Lo and Amherstburg. The ferries, a full service restaurant, the 110-slip marina, a fudge shop and a small store are all open to the public.

Mr. Oram estimates that full development of the island residential community will take 30 years. Bill Browning, Executive Vice President and General Manager of the Bob-Lo companies for 30 years, said they had considered building summer cottages on Bob-Lo that families would rent for a week or more. The inadequate road that existed at that time between Windsor and Amherstburg was an important reason that the project never got off the ground. Browning was enthusiastic about the new real estate development, "The project is admirable and imaginative. John Oram is doing a fantastic job. I hope he is successful beyond his dreams. He's building a Mackinac Island 30 minutes from Detroit."[42]

A herd of 30 deer also lives and prospers on the Island. They have been there since before 1994. Those familiar with the area speculate that the deer found their way to Bob-Lo from Michigan on the frozen river. Part of the old lighthouse and one of the 1838 blockhouses still stand on the south end of Bob-Lo. The impressions made on the ground by the roller coaster structure and other rides can still be seen, and the Sky Tower and pizza carryout shack are still there along with the cut stone dance pavilion and the roller rink. The old power plant building, designed to resemble a chapel, is now occasionally used for weddings. As recently as July 2002, the former petting farm was home for a male emu and a female Shetland pony. Marcella Collins, an employee of the Bob-Lo Island Resort Community, provides for their care and feeding. A fan of 1930s movie musicals, she told me, "They are named Fred and Ginger, but I never saw them dance."[43]

Residence on Bob-Lo Island, July 2002

THE BOATS AND THE AMUSEMENT PARK ARE GONE NOW, and the Detroit metropolitan area is the lesser for the loss. A new generation grows up knowing Bob-Lo only through the stories of their parents and grandparents. Frank Stodgell captured the good feeling that Bob-Lo gave in his "Bob-Lo Song," written in 1913:

> *I say take a trip*
> *To old Bob-Lo*
> *Where the boys and girls*
> *Delight to go.*
>
> *Then home, sweet home,*
> *From old Bob-Lo,*
> *In the evening*
> *When the sun is low.*
>
> *It's a beautiful ride*
> *By the light of the moon,*
> *Dancing home to a rag-time tune.*

End Notes

1. *Detroit Sunday News-Tribune*, June 5, 1898.
2. *Detroit Evening News*, June 9, 1898.
3. *Detroit News*, August 27, 1959.
4. *Detroit Free Press*, ca. 1900, reprinted July 31, 1967.
5. *Detroit Free Press*, June 5, 1958.
6. Bob-Lo Island Pictorial Booklet, published by Island of Bob-Lo Company, A John Hinde Curteich Inc. Product, ca 1980.
7. *Detroit Free Press*, October 20, 1958; *Windsor Star*, September 12, 1958.
8. *Detroit News*, June 18, 1940.
9. *Border Cities Star*, June 4, 1921.
10. Weld, Isaac, Jr., *Travels Through the States of North America, and the Provinces of Upper and Lower Canada, During the Years 1795, 1796, and 1797* (London, 1799).
11. *Amherstburg Echo*, March 1, 1901.
12. Gary Sodini interview, September 30, 2000.
13. *Detroit Free Press*, March 2, 1987.
14. Anon., *Amherstburg 1796-1976: The New Town on the Garrison Grounds, Book II* (Marsh Collection Society, Amherstburg, 1997) at 280, hereafter *Amherstburg*.
15. *Detroit Free Press*, August 4, 1978.
16. Jack Harris interview, September 8, 2000.
17. *Detroit Free Press*, September 16, 1999.
18. Jane McCraight-Wertz interview, August 22, 2002.
19. *Detroit Free Press*, December 25, 1974.
20. Ralph Browning interview, September 4, 2002.
21. *Detroit Free Press*, September 7, 1970.
22. Undated article, 1906 scrapbook, Dossin Great Lakes Museum, Detroit.
23. Ralph Browning interview, September 4, 2002.
24. *Detroit News*, July 9, 1973.
25. *Amherstburg* 138.
26. *Detroit News*, August 27, 1959.
27. *Detroit Free Press*, June 13. 1948.
28. *Detroit Free Press*, December 5, 1997.
29. *Bob-Lo Excursion Co. v. Michigan*, 333 U.S. 28, 35(1948).
30. *Detroit Free Press*, May 21, 1949.
31. Ralph and Bill Browning interviews, September 2002.
32. Jane Davies-Culp interview, September 30, 2002.
33. Jane Davies-Culp interviews, September 30 and October 2, 2002.
34. *Detroit News*, February 25, 1990.
35. Gary Sodini interview, September 30, 2000.
36. Jane McCraight-Wertz interview, August 22, 2002.
37. Ralph Browning interview, September 4, 2002.

38. Diane Evon interview, October 2, 2002.

39. Letter to The Friends of the Bob-Lo Boat *Columbia* from the National Trust for Historic Preservation, January 8, 2003, at http://www.steamercolumbia.org/fax.jpg, January 21, 2003; telephone interview with Krista Kendall, Program Associate, National Trust for Historic Preservation, January 21, 2003.

40. Indian Claims Commission, Government of Canada, *Walpole Island First Nation Inquiry, Bob-Lo Island Claim*, decided May 2000, at 87-88, website http://www.indianclaims.ca/english/pub/claimsreports.html, December 11, 2002; *Detroit News*, May 15, 2000.

41. Walpole Island First Nation, Press Release, May 11, 2000, at website http://www.bkejwanong.com/sombra/BobLo_release.htm, December 11, 2002.

42. Bill Browning interview, September 13, 2002.

43. Marcella Collins interview, July 29, 2002.

Select Bibliography

Amherstburg Echo, April 1898-November 1959.

Amherstburg 1796-1976: The New Town on the Garrison Grounds, Book II. Amherstburg: Marsh Collection Society, 1997.

Bob-Lo Excursion Co. v. Michigan, 333 U.S. 28 (1948).

Island of Bob-Lo Company. *Bob-Lo Island Amusement Park*. 1981.

Island of Bob-Lo Company. *Group Outing*. 1992.

Coaster Enthusiasts of Canada. website: cec.chebucto.org

Crain's Detroit Business, December 18, 2000.

Creed, J.A.,ed., *Bob-Lo: A Tiny Canadian Island*. Windsor: Herald Press Ltd., 1987.

Cumming, John. "Revolution in the Wilderness: Michigan as Colony and Territory." In *Michigan: Visions of our Past,* edited by Richard J. Hathaway. East Lansing: Michigan State University Press, 1989.

Detroit Free Press, 19 November 1901- 9 October 2001.

Detroit Journal, 12 May 1898-27 February 1906.

Detroit Monitor, 13 March 1986 -19 October 1995.

Detroit News, 5 June 1898 -14 September 2000.

Detroit News-Tribune, 5 June 1898.

Detroit Times, 6 July 1956.

Glenn Black Laboratory of Archaeology and Trustees of Indiana University. website: www.gbl.indiana.edu

Indian Claims Commission, Government of Canada, Decision of May 1, 2000.

Michigan Historical Center. website: www.michigan.gov/hal

Moffett, William A., *The Story of Bob-Lo Island*. Detroit: Bob-Lo Excursion Co., n.d.

New Center News, 19 October 1998.

Parke, Davis & Co. misc. brochures. 4 June 1902; 13 June 1905.

Roller Coaster Almanac. website: www.rollercoaster.com/resources/almanac

Schoolcraft, Henry R. "Narrative Journal of Travels Through the Northwestern Regions of the United States ."(1820) In *Schoolcraft's Narrative Journal of Travels*, edited by Mentor L. Williams. East Lansing: Michigan State University Press, 1992.

University of Windsor. website: http://athena.uwindsor.ca

Smith, W.H. *Canada Past, Present and Future*. n.p., 1852.

Walpole Island First Nation. website: www.bkejwanong.com

Weld, Isaac, Jr. *Travels Through the States of North America, and the Provinces of Upper and Lower Canada, during the Years 1795, 1796, and 1797*. London: n.p., 1799.

Windsor Evening Record, 30 July 1904-7 June 1913.

Windsor Star, 12 September, 1958; 31 May 1988; 26 February 1990; 9 March 1994.

ACKNOWLEDGEMENTS

I am grateful for the help and resources of the following institutions and organizations: Baldwin Public Library, Birmingham, Michigan; Bentley Historical Library, University of Michigan, Ann Arbor; Bloomfield Township Library, Bloomfield Hills, Michigan; Burton Historical Collection and History and Travel Department, Detroit Public Library; Coaster Enthusiasts of Canada; *Detroit Free Press* Archives; *Detroit News* Archives; Dossin Great Lakes Museum, Detroit, Michigan; Heritage Centre, Walpole Island First Nation; Indian Claims Commission, Government of Canada; Marsh Collection Society, Amherstburg, Ontario; Michigan Historical Center, Lansing, Michigan; Tricentennial Committee of Windsor, Ontario; University of Windsor Library and the Windsor Public Library, Windsor, Ontario; Wayne State University Law Library, Detroit, Michigan.

I am especially indebted to the gracious cooperation of those
who agreed to participate in interviews for this history:

John Belko

Bill Browning

Helen Mayhew Browning

Ralph Browning

Marcella Collins

Jane Davies-Culp

Diane Evon

Jack Harris

Krista Kendall

Jane McCraight-Wertz

Bill Rohrer

Gary Sondini

– Martin Magid, April 2003

Printed by University Lithoprinters, Inc., Ann Arbor, Michigan
Bound by Dekker Bookbinding, Grand Rapids, Michigan
Paper: Luna Matte 100# text
Type set in Dante by Press Lorentz,
Ann Arbor / Chicago